Kanye West

by C.F. Earl

Superstars of Hip-Hop

Kanye West

by C.F. Earl

Mason Crest

Kanye West

Mason Crest
370 Reed Road
Broomall, Pennsylvania 19008
www.masoncrest.com

Printed and bound in the United States of America.

First printing
9 8 7 6 5 4 3 2 1

Library of Congress Cataloging-in-Publication Data

Earl, C. F.
  Kanye West / by C.F. Earl.
      p. cm. – (Superstars of hip-hop)
  Includes index.
  ISBN 978-1-4222-2533-2 (hardcover) – ISBN 978-1-4222-2508-0 (series hardcover) – ISBN 978-1-4222-2559-2 (softcover) – ISBN 978-1-4222-9235-8 (ebook)
 1. West, Kanye–Juvenile literature. 2. Rap musicians–United States–Biography–Juvenile literature. I. Title.
  ML3930.W42E27 2012
  782.421649092–dc22
  [B]
                                2011005808

Produced by Harding House Publishing Services, Inc.
www.hardinghousepages.com
Interior Design by MK Bassett-Harvey.
Cover design by Torque Advertising & Design.

Publisher's notes:
- All quotations in this book come from original sources and contain the spelling and grammatical inconsistencies of the original text.
- The Web sites mentioned in this book were active at the time of publication. The publisher is not responsible for Web sites that have changed their addresses or discontinued operation since the date of publication. The publisher will review and update the Web site addresses each time the book is reprinted.

DISCLAIMER: The following story has been thoroughly researched, and to the best of our knowledge, represents a true story. While every possible effort has been made to ensure accuracy, the publisher will not assume liability for damages caused by inaccuracies in the data, and makes no warranty on the accuracy of the information contained herein. This story has not been authorized nor endorsed by Kanye West.

Contents

Hip-Hop lingo

A **recording** is a sound or video that has been saved on a computer or a CD.

A **producer** is the person in charge of putting together songs. A producer makes the big decisions about the music.

Beats are the basic rhythms or pulse of a piece of music.

An **album** is a group of songs collected together on a CD.

Chapter 1

Where It All Began

Today, Kanye West is one of rap's biggest stars. His music has touched millions of people. His songs can be heard on the radio and on TV. You can see his face in magazines and on websites.

Few artists are as loved and hated as Kanye West. He's reached great heights with his music. But he's also made people angry about the things he's said in public. Like him or not, Kanye West seems to be everywhere.

Kanye's life wasn't always so amazing. He was just like a lot of other kids growing up. He had big dreams, though. He didn't just want to become a rapper. He wanted to be the biggest, best rapper that ever lived.

Dreaming Big

Kanye Omari West was born on June 8, 1977 in Atlanta, Georgia. His mother, Dr. Donda West, was an English professor. In Atlanta, she taught English at Clark Atlanta University. Kanye's father, Ray West, was a photographer for a newspaper.

THE BLACK PANTHER
INTERCOMMUNAL NEWS SERVICE
PUBLISHED WEEKLY BY THE BLACK PANTHER PARTY

COPYRIGHT © 1977, by Huey P. Newton   VOL. XVI NO. 16   SATURDAY, FEBRUARY 26, 1977   25¢

Inside

- **Elaine Brown Honored By Fremont High School Students**
  RECEIVES PLAQUE AT AFRO-AMERICAN HISTORY ASSEMBLY   PAGE 3

- **Athletes Endorse Judge Wilson For Mayor Of Oakland**
  TOP PRESENT, FORMER PROFESSIONAL SPORTSMEN HOLD PRESS CONFERENCE   PAGE 7

- **FRELIMO Reorganizes As A Vanguard Political Party**
  SAMORA MACHEL CALLS FOR "IRON ORGANIZATION AND DISCIPLINE"   CENTERFOLD

- **Foreign Leaders Bribed With C.I.A. Payoffs**
  PROJECT "NO BEEF" EXPOSES PAYMENTS TO DOZENS OF HEADS OF STATE   PAGE 17

Oakland Community School Performance

"REMEMBERING OUR ROOTS" CELEBRATES BLACK HISTORY

(Oakland, Calif.) — In celebration of Black History Month, the talented children of the Oakland Community School (OCS) presented an original five-act play entitled *Remembering Our Roots* on Sunday, February 20, at the Oakland Community Learning Center.

Following a welcome from OCS Director Ericka Huggins, *Remembering Our Roots* got underway. The play was appropriately named as it traced the history of Black people in America from their abduction from Africa into slavery up to the present. As is always the case for OCS productions, the play was written by the children themselves.

The play was presented as an "Oakland Community School News Special," and news commentators were Jackie Logan, Walter Butler and Glen Thornton. Jackie began by explaining that the history of Black Americans started in Africa.

Next, the boys and girls of Levels 4-7, ages six through 11, presented an Azanian (South African) warrior chant and dance that is used as a warning in a test of skills. The children received several rounds of applause from the audience during their polished performance of the warrior dance, taught to them by the creative OCS Artist-in-Residence, Ms. Thoko-Mordlase Hall, whose home is Azania.

Following the warrior dance, the girls of Levels 4-7 performed another Azanian chant and dance. The young sisters' rhythmic, soulful movements across the stage reminded everyone present of the roots of Black
CONTINUED ON PAGE 6

Oakland Community School Director ERICKA HUGGINS (above) and scenes from the School's special Black history celebration held last Sunday.

BPNS photos

Kanye's father, Ray was a member of the Black Panthers. Active from the late 1960s to early 1970s, the Black Panthers was a controversial African American political group. Its goal was to end white domination and better the lives of African Americans.

Kanye was three years old when his parents split up. Kanye and his mom moved to Chicago. Donda started teaching at Chicago State University. Kanye spent summers with his dad in Atlanta.

Kanye loved to entertain people. When he was ten, he and his mother moved to China for a year. Donda worked at Nanjing University. When he lived in China, Kanye would entertain people on the street. He'd try to earn some money for ice cream. He'd show off his martial arts moves to anyone who wanted to watch.

After he moved back to the United States, kids teased Kanye for having lived in China. They called him names like "China Boy." But Kanye didn't care. By then, his love for entertaining people had focused on music.

Kanye was thirteen when he recorded his first song. It was called "Green Eggs and Ham." To make the **recording**, he had to convince his mom to give him $25.

Then, Kanye talked his mom into lending him money for a keyboard. He was making more and more music. He started to go to concerts and clubs to see hip-hop artists perform.

When Kanye was fourteen, Donda met another teacher whose son was making music. Donda asked the other woman to introduce her son to Kanye. Donda knew Kanye was really getting into music. She thought he could use some help and advice. The other teacher's son was **producer** No I.D. No I.D. was known for working with Chicago rapper Common.

When Kanye met No I.D., he was excited to learn everything he could about producing. No I.D. was older than Kanye. He thought maybe the younger boy was going to be trouble for him. But after a while, No I.D. saw that Kanye was learning a lot. He was becoming very good at making music.

No I.D. kept teaching Kanye things about producing songs. Kanye learned more and more. He used what he learned to make music.

Kanye dreamed of being a great rapper. He dreamed of being the next big thing in hip-hop. Kanye knew he wanted to make music. He just had to make it happen.

Run-DMC was one of hip-hop's earliest and biggest success stories. Shown in this 2001 photo are (left to right) Darryl (DMC) McDaniel, Joseph (Run) Simmons, and Jason (Jam Master Jay) Mizell. Jam Master Jay was murdered in a shooting outside a recording studio in 2002.

Kanye Drops Out

Kanye graduated from Polaris High School. He did well in school, too. Education was very important to his mother and father. His mom had been a university professor all Kanye's life. His father had two degrees and also taught Kanye about the importance of education.

When Kanye was finished with high school, he started taking classes at an art school in Chicago. He also took classes at Chicago State University. Kanye was still focused on music, though.

Kanye knew education was important to his family. He knew his parents wanted him to stay in school and do well. But Kanye also wanted to follow his dreams. School was taking up time he wanted to be using on his music. So, after a year of college, Kanye spoke to his mother about leaving school.

He told her that he would take one year to go after his dream. He would try for one year to make it in the music world. Donda didn't like that her son would be leaving college without getting a degree. But she knew Kanye needed to be free to do what he wanted. Kanye talked his mom into letting him take a chance on his music.

Kanye started working during the day so he could pay his mother rent. She knew it was important to have him pull his own weight in their house. It was also a way to teach Kanye how to manage his money and be responsible.

After working his day job, Kanye went home and worked another sort of job. At night, Kanye stayed up working on his music. He made **beats** for other rappers. He worked on his production skills. He was also focusing on becoming a better rapper.

After a few months of working during the day and making music at night, Kanye had his first success. He sold some beats to

After much soul-searching, Kanye decided to quit college to pursue his music career. This doesn't mean he thinks everyone should be a dropout, though. Kanye participates in many programs that encourage kids to stay in school and get an education.

Chicago rapper Gravity. Kanye ended up producing eight songs for Gravity's first **album**, *Down to Earth*. The album came out in 1996.

Over the next few years, Kanye started producing songs for bigger and bigger artists. He still dreamed of becoming a rapper. He wanted to rap on songs as well as produce them. But Kanye was also happy to finally be making music. He hadn't reached all of his goals, but he was on his way.

Hip-Hop lingo

A **single** is a song that is sold by itself.

A **studio** is a place where musicians go to record their music and turn it into CDs.

When a voice is **high-pitched,** it can be shrill and squeaky.

Mixtapes are collections of a few songs put on a CD or given away for free on the Internet without being professionally recorded.

The **singles chart** is a list of the best-selling songs for a week.

Critics are people who judge artistic works and say what is good and what is bad about them.

Each year, the National Academy of Recording Arts and Sciences gives out the Grammy Awards (short for Gramophone Awards)—or **Grammys**—to people who have done something really big in the music industry.

When someone has been **nominated,** he has been picked as one of the people who might win an award.

Chapter 2

Breakthrough

Day by day, Kanye was working his way toward his dreams. He knew that by working hard, he could reach his goals. He knew he could become the rapper he dreamed of being.

Kanye's plan of taking a year to work on his music had changed. Now, he was close to making his dreams come true. He just needed to keep at it a little longer. He needed to work as hard as he could.

Kanye, the Producer

By the late '90s, Kanye was starting to work with bigger artists. In 1998, he helped produce for Jermaine Dupri and Foxy Brown. In 1999, he worked on the first album from Ma$e's group Harlem World. He also produced a song called "Rebuilding," for the group Goodie Mob. The song was on the group's 1999 album, *World Party*.

Kanye's biggest break as a producer came from rapper Jay-Z and his company Roc-A-Fella Records.

In 2000, Kanye produced a song called "This Can't Be Life." The song was for Jay-Z's album *The Dynasty: Roc La Familia*. It was the only song that Kanye produced for the album. It was the start of something much bigger, though.

After *The Dynasty* came out, Kanye knew he could make it in music. He knew he could keep doing what he wanted to be doing. He moved to New York City to start working on music full-time.

In 2001, Kanye produced four tracks for Jay-Z's *The Blueprint*. The album came out on September 11, 2001. It was a huge success. Its **single** "Izzo (H.O.V.A.)" was very popular. Kanye had produced that song. After *The Blueprint*, lots of artists wanted to work with Kanye. They'd heard his work and knew he had talent.

Kanye started working for more artists. He was producing more songs than he ever had before. He worked with Nas, Scarface, Talib Kweli, and many others.

Kanye had become very successful as a producer. But no one saw him as a rapper. He wanted to make his own beats and rap over them.

Jay-Z had helped Kanye get where he was. The New York rapper had given Kanye a chance to make songs with great artists. But now that Kanye wanted to become an artist, Jay-Z wasn't so sure it was the right move.

Kanye didn't look like most other rappers. He wore bright colors. He wore polo shirts. Many companies—even Roc-a-Fella—thought it would be too hard to sell a rapper like Kanye. They weren't sure he could be successful as an artist.

Kanye talked to lots of different record companies. But no one thought Kanye would be successful. When Kanye talked about wanting to move on, Roc-A-Fella finally signed a deal with him. They wanted to keep Kanye producing songs for them. But they still weren't sure he could be the next big thing in rap.

In 2002, Kanye worked on Jay-Z's *The Blueprint 2: The Gift and the Curse.* He produced another four tracks for the album. He also got to rap on a song called "The Bounce."

One of Kanye's biggest breaks as a produceer came when he caught the attention of hip-hop legend Jay-Z, shown here with Kanye in 2005. According to Kanye, working on Jay-Z's "Izzo (H.O.V.A.)" was a "turning point" in his life and career.

Kanye's career as a producer for Jay-Z's record company, Rock-A-Fella, was nothing short of a monumental success. Major hip-hop stars wanted him to produce their music. Eventually, Rock-A-Fella signed him to record his own music. Former clients, such as Twista (right), became fellow performers.

For many people, it was the first time they heard Kanye rap. They might have known him as a producer, but not as a rapper.

Now, Kanye was on his way to becoming the rapper he'd always wanted to be. He'd gotten a record deal with Roc-A-Fella. He finally had a chance at his dream.

A Close Call and Second Chance

By 2002, Kanye's future was bright. He was working with some of the biggest rappers in the world. He'd made his way into the music world, and people loved the tracks he made. Kanye was working as hard as he ever had. But then he had a close call. It showed Kanye that everything could be gone in a second.

In October 2002, Kanye was driving home. He'd been spending lots of time working in the recording **studio**. He was working hard. He'd spent hours and hours making music. Kanye had tired himself out. He fell asleep while driving and crashed his car.

The car crash was a close call for Kanye. He survived. He was hurt badly, though. The crash could have killed him.

Kanye was taken to the hospital. He had to have surgery on his face. His jaw was wired shut. The wires kept Kanye's mouth from moving while his jaw healed. He could still talk, but his words weren't as clear. This was especially upsetting for someone who wanted to use his voice to make a living.

The car crash had a big effect on Kanye. He felt it was a reminder of how quickly things can change. His life had been going so well. But if things had gone differently during the crash, he might have lost everything. Kanye felt like he had a second chance. And he was going to use his chance to make his own music.

While Kanye was in the hospital, he started working on a song about the crash. Three weeks later, he was in the studio. With his jaw still wired shut, Kanye rapped verses for a song called "Though the Wire." Kanye's voice didn't sound like it normally did because of the wiring. But he was still able to get across his feelings.

"Through the Wire" showed off Kanye's production style. Its beat was based on the 1985 Chaka Khan song "Though the Fire."

An almost-fatal car accident in 2002 was life changing for Kanye. It caused him to reflect on the "what might have been" and the "what could be" of his career—and more important, of his life.

Kanye took "Though the Fire" and sped up the singer's voice. That made it sounded very **high-pitched**.

"Through the Wire" was released as a single on September 30, 2003. Before then, the song came out on unofficial **mixtapes**. When the song came out, it was number ninety-four on the **singles chart**. Soon, it reached number fifteen. The song was a big hit for a new artist.

Roc-A-Fella saw the success of "Through the Wire." The song was popular enough that they agreed to put out Kanye's first album.

It was finally time for Kanye to move from being a producer to being a rapper. He had finally convinced the people who didn't think he could make it. Now, Roc-A-Fella was ready to put out his first album.

Kanye, the Rapper

Kanye had been working on songs for his first album for a few years before it came out. He'd make beats and work on songs for other artists. Then he'd go home and work on his own music. Many of the songs were recorded in Kanye's bedroom.

Kanye called his album *The College Dropout*. It came out on February 10, 2004.

"Through the Wire" was the first single from *The College Dropout*. It came out a few months before the album. The song helped to get people excited for *The College Dropout*. It also gave people a taste of the album's sound.

While "Through the Wire" was on the charts, another Kanye song was also becoming very popular. The song was called "Slow Jamz." It featured rapper Twista and singer Jaime Foxx. "Slow Jamz" was on Twista's album *Kamikaze* and on *The College Dropout*. Just before *The College Dropout* came out, the song was number one on the singles chart.

The next single from *The College Dropout* was called "All Falls Down." The song was a big hit for Kanye, though it didn't reach number one. "All Falls Down" made it to number seven, though. It was Kanye's biggest hit on his own so far.

After "All Falls Down," Kanye released the single "Jesus

Is Kanye West outrageous? Maybe. But, he always puts on a good show. Kanye is shown here performing his hit "Jesus Walks" at the 47th Annual Grammy Awards in 2005. "Jesus Walks" won the Grammy for

the charts. It was a big hit with **critics**, though. They thought the song showed a lot of Kanye's skills. They liked its sound.

Many critics also liked that the song was about different things than many rap songs. On "Jesus Walks," Kanye rapped about religion and his own faith.

The College Dropout was a hit. In its first week out, the album sold more 440,000 copies. *The College Dropout* was the number-two album in the country the week it was released.

At the 2005 **Grammys**, Kanye was **nominated** for ten awards. Some of Kanye's nominations were for songs he'd worked on for other artists. But he won two for his own music. Kanye won Best Rap Album for *The College Dropout*. He also won Best Rap Song for "Jesus Walks." Kanye performed the song at the awards show, too. Kanye also won a Grammy for his work on Alicia Keys' "You Don't Know My Name."

Kanye West had reached his goal. He was the rapper he'd always wanted to be. His album had sold millions of copies. His songs were on the radio. His videos were on TV. Kanye's music seemed to be everywhere.

Hip-Hop lingo

Soundtracks are collections of all the songs on a movie.

Chapter 3

Kanye Goes His Own Way

The College Dropout made Kanye a star. Songs like "All Falls Down" and "Jesus Walks" were huge hits. His music was on the radio. His videos were on TV. He was working with lots of other artists, too. It seemed like Kanye was everywhere.

He'd gone from unknown producer to rap star in just a couple of years. But Kanye wasn't about to slow down. He started work on his next album.

Late Registration

Kanye's new album was called *Late Registration*. It had a different sound than *The College Dropout*. Kanye felt that his style of production was being used more and more by other artists. He wanted to do something different. He also wanted to keep getting better at making music.

To help produce the album, Kanye brought in composer Jon Brion. Brion had worked on many movie **soundtracks**. He helped Kanye include more instruments in his music.

Late Registration was released on August 30, 2005. Fans had been waiting for the album. They were excited to hear Kanye's new songs.

Late Registration's first single was "Diamonds from Sierra Leone." It came out a few months before the album. The second single was called "Gold Digger." Jaime Foxx sang the chorus of

According to critics, Kanye's star appeal isn't the only thing that is super-sized—so is his ego. However, Kanye always remembers his fans. Here, he is autographing copies of his 2005 release *Late Registration* for fans in a New York City record store.

the song, which was taken from a Ray Charles song. "Gold Digger" was a giant hit. The song spent ten weeks at number one on the singles chart.

The third single was "Heard 'Em Say." Adam Levine, singer for the band Maroon 5, sang the chorus of the song. The next single was "Touch the Sky." Both songs did well, but nowhere near as well as "Gold Digger."

The last single from *Late Registration* was called "Drive Slow." It featured rappers Paul Wall and GLC.

In its first week out, *Late Registration* was the number-one album in the United States. It sold 860,000 copies that week. The album sold almost three million copies in the United States in one year.

At the 2006 Grammys, Kanye was nominated for eight awards. He won three. He won Best Rap Album for *Late Registration*. He also won Best Rap Song for "Diamonds from Sierra Leone." And he won Best Rap Solo Performance for "Gold Digger."

With *Late Registration*, Kanye proved that *The College Dropout* wasn't just luck. Many artists find their second album isn't as successful as their first. This wasn't true with Kanye. His second album was even bigger than his first.

Graduation

Kanye's third album was called *Graduation*. The album came out on September 11, 2007.

Kanye wanted to change his sound again for this album. He wanted to make sure he wasn't doing the same songs over and over. He wanted to make sure his music was always growing and moving forward.

Kanye studied rock bands like Led Zeppelin and the Rolling Stones. He wanted to make hip-hop music sound as big as rock music did in stadiums. He wanted big choruses and big hooks.

Graduation had a few big hit singles. They helped make the album such a success. They also helped keep Kanye on the radio and on TV for another year.

The first single from *Graduation* was "Can't Tell Me Nothing." The song came out a few months before the album. "Can't Tell Me Nothing" wasn't played much on the radio. The video wasn't

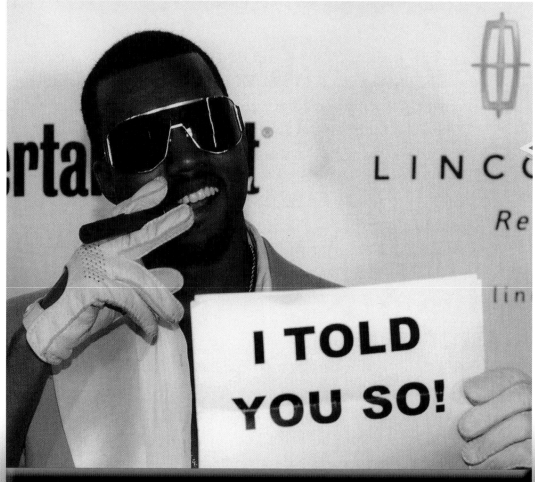

Kanye had predicted he would win at the 2006 Grammys— and sure enough, he did (although he did not win Album of the Year as he had hoped). At a post-Grammy party, Kanye took the opportunity to gloat just a little on camera.

played on TV much, either. But Kanye was still proud of the song. Critics liked it, too.

The album's second single was "Stronger." The beat for "Stronger" takes parts of a Daft Punk song called "Harder, Better, Faster, Stronger." "Stronger" was the first big hit from *Graduation*. The song reached number one on the singles chart. The song was played on radio and TV a lot. It was played in clubs around the country.

The third single was "Good Life," featuring T-Pain. "Flashing Lights" was the fourth single. "Flashing Lights" was a hit on the charts. It was also used in the video game, *Grand Theft Auto 4*. "Flashing Lights" was one of the biggest hits from *Graduation*.

Graduation was another big success for Kanye. The album sold almost a million copies in its first week out. It was also the number-one album in the country that week.

At the 2008 Grammys, Kanye was nominated for eight awards. He won Best Rap Song for "Good Life." He won Best Solo Rap Performance for "Stronger." He also won Best Rap Album for *Graduation*. And, he won Best Rap Performance by a Duo or Group for Common's "Southside."

Kanye had reached heights that most artists dream about. He was selling millions of albums. He was winning awards and gaining fans. Few artists were as famous as Kanye West had become. The boy who dreamed of being the world's biggest rapper had gotten his wish.

Hip-Hop lingo

When someone has **dedicated** a song or performance to another person, he performs it in her honor.

Controversial means causing a lot of people to argue, disagree, or get upset.

Chapter 4

Death in the Family

It seemed as though Kanye's life couldn't get any better. He'd become one of rap's biggest stars. His three albums were huge hits. They had sold millions of copies. Kanye had won many awards, too. But his life was about to take a turn for the worse.

Kanye Loses His Mother

In November 2007, Donda West died after surgery. Her funeral was held on November 20, in Oklahoma City. At the funeral, Kanye said a few words. He was too sad to say much. He said he knew his mother would want him to get up and speak, though.

Two days later, Kanye performed in London. During the show, Kanye **dedicated** "Hey Mama" to his mother. He told the crowd that his mother was his first fan. He said she liked to come to his shows and scream as loud as she could. Kanye said his mother always taught him to do the best he could.

With his mother gone, Kanye had lost one of his biggest supporters. His mother had always been a big part of his life. She'd taught him

In a repeat of 2005, Kanye won three Grammy Awards in 2006. Here he is shown sharing the spotlight with his girlfriend (center) and mother(right). Kanye's mother, Donda West, was a big influence on his success—and life.

about the importance of education. She'd helped him get started in music. She'd supported him when it seemed no one else was on his side. Donda had even worked as Kanye's manager. She had always been there for Kanye. And now she was gone.

Through 2008, Kanye kept on working. He began his Glow In the Dark Tour in April. The tour lasted from April until December. First, Kanye traveled across the United States. Then, he went to Brazil, China, Europe, and Australia. Kanye was busy with the tour for most of the year.

Traveling so much made relationships difficult. Kanye and his girlfriend, Alexis Phifer, had been together since 2002. Kanye asked Alexis to marry him in 2006. But with Kanye gone on tour for almost eight months, the couple just couldn't stay together. Kanye and Alexis broke up.

Kanye had lost his mother and his girlfriend in a year's time. They had helped guide him through his rise to success. They'd been there when no one else had been. Now Kanye was on his own.

808s and Heartbreak

Kanye went to work on his next album. He wanted to express how he was feeling. He wanted to make music that sounded as lonely as he felt. He wanted his next album to sound different from other hip-hop albums. He also wanted it to sound different from his other albums.

Kanye decided to use a drum machine called a Roland TR-808. He thought the drum sound the machine made matched the lonely feeling he wanted for the new album.

To match the cold, electronic drum sound, Kanye wanted to change the way he recorded his voice, too. Kanye decided that he would use a machine to change his voice for the new album. A program called Auto-Tune had been used on lots of rap and pop songs. But Kanye thought he could use it better than others.

Kanye named his new album *808s & Heartbreak*. It was released on November 24, 2008.

Kanye introduced his new sound in September 2008. At the 2008 MTV Video Music Awards, he performed a new song. The song was called "Love Lockdown." The song had no rapping in it. Instead, Kanye sang the whole song.

"Love Lockdown" was a big change for Kanye fans. They knew Kanye as a rapper. They didn't know him as a singer. The song gave fans a taste of what they could expect from the new album. Some people loved the new sound. Others felt it wasn't like Kanye at all.

Kanye didn't want people to look at his new album in the same way as his other albums. He told fans that *808s & Heartbreak* wasn't a rap album. It was a pop album, he said. Kanye said that he didn't like that some people thought pop music couldn't be good.

The album's second single was "Heartless." The third was called "Amazing." Rapper Young Jeezy performed a verse on "Amazing." At the 2010 Grammys, the song was nominated for Best Rap Performance by a Duo or Group. *808s & Heartbreak*'s final single was called "Paranoid." English rock artist Mr. Hudson was featured on the song.

808s & Heartbreak was a hit for Kanye. But it wasn't as big a hit as *Graduation*. In its first week out, *808s & Heartbreak* sold around 450,000 copies. The album was also number one in the country during its first week.

808s & Heartbreak was very different from Kanye's other music. The album was Kanye's way of expressing himself. After losing his mother and his fiancée, Kanye had been at a low point in his life. *808s* was his way of dealing with that pain. Kanye used his music as a way to get his feelings out.

The change in Kanye's sound and style wasn't for everyone, though. Some people thought *808s & Heartbreak* was a mistake. They thought Kanye should stick to rapping.

808s & Heartbreak was **controversial** in the music world. But that controversy was nothing compared to what lay ahead.

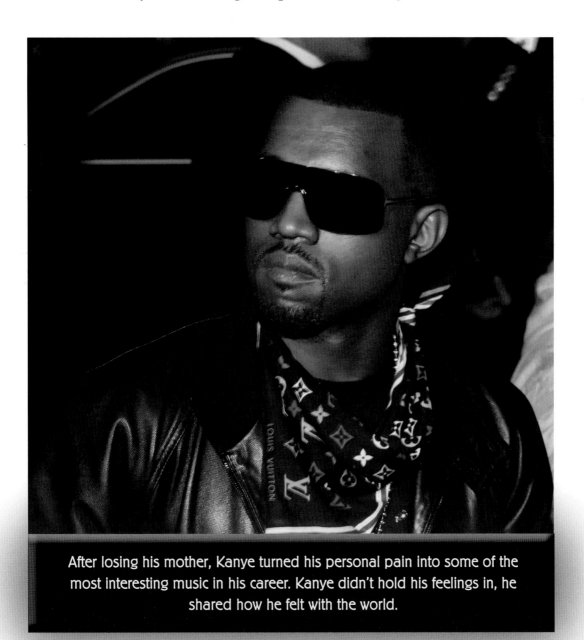

After losing his mother, Kanye turned his personal pain into some of the most interesting music in his career. Kanye didn't hold his feelings in, he shared how he felt with the world.

Controversy Follows Kanye

In September 2009, Kanye went to the MTV Video Music Awards. Country singer Taylor Swift won the Best Female Video award for her "You Belong With Me" music video.

When the award for Best Female Video was announced, Kanye didn't think the decision was right. Kanye thought Beyoncé should have won for her song "Single Ladies." He ran on stage and took the microphone from Swift as she was accepting the award. He told the crowd that Beyoncé had the better video. He said she should have won the award instead of Taylor.

The audience was shocked. They weren't sure if it was a joke or if it had been planned. Some people even laughed. But it wasn't a joke. Kanye had just interrupted Taylor Swift's speech. Kanye wasn't allowed to stay for the rest of the show. MTV asked him to leave.

Later that night, Beyoncé won the Video of the Year award for "Single Ladies." She called Swift to come up to the stage and give her speech again.

Kanye knew he'd made a mistake. He still thought Beyoncé should have won the award. But he knew he shouldn't have interrupted Taylor's speech. Kanye knew he needed to apologize. He wrote on his blog that night about how sorry he was.

The next day, Kanye went on *The Jay Leno Show* to apologize to Taylor. He told Jay he was going to take some time off to think about what he'd done. He told the audience that what he'd done wasn't right. "It was rude, period," he said.

After the VMAs, lots of people were talking about Kanye. Most people weren't happy about his actions. They thought he'd been mean. They called Kanye names. Lots of artists who'd been there said they were very angry that Kanye had messed up Taylor's speech. Even President Barack Obama said he thought Kanye was wrong.

Kanye decided he should leave the United States to get away. First, he moved to Japan for a few weeks to be alone. After that, he moved to Rome, Italy. There, he started working for a fashion company called Fendi.

Kanye had come a long way since he started in music. He'd gained fans around the world. But now Kanye felt something he'd never really felt before. He felt like people didn't like him. He felt like people didn't want him around.

Hip-Hop lingo

A **phoenix** is a mythical bird that lives for hundreds of years, then burns itself up. It comes out of the ashes of the fire, young again, then lives for hundreds more years.

Chapter 5

Kanye's Beautiful Dark Twisted Fantasy

By 2010, Kanye was ready to come back to the United States. He was ready to start on his next album. He knew his new album needed to be something special. He wanted to show people his talent. Even if they didn't like him. He wanted his music to do his talking for him.

Kanye traveled to Hawaii. He started to work on the new album with his friends. Kanye wanted to make a great album. He wanted to add something special to the history of hip-hop. He also wanted to prove he could make a come back.

My Beautiful Dark Twisted Fantasy

For months, no one was sure what Kanye was working on. He wasn't seen in public much. He wasn't putting out new songs. But then, Kanye came out of hiding. He'd been hard at work. He wanted to show people what he was working on.

On July 1, 2010, Kanye put out the first single from his new album. The song was called "Power." It was the first song fans had heard in a long time. Then, at the 2010 Video Music Awards in September,

Kanye performed another new song. Wearing a bright red suit, Kanye performed "Runaway." Pusha T rapped a verse on the song. It was another taste of Kanye's new album.

By October, Kanye's fans still didn't know what the album was called. On October 4, Kanye announced the new album would be called *My Beautiful Dark Twisted Fantasy*. The album came out on November 26, 2010.

Before the album came out, Kanye made a thirty-minute music video to go along with "Runaway." Kanye directed the video himself. The video is like a short movie. It tells the story of a **phoenix** that falls to Earth and meets Kanye. Kanye and the phoenix fall in love. But she can't stay with Kanye because she doesn't fit into his human world. The video has many songs from *My Beautiful Dark Twisted Fantasy*.

The third single from the album was "Monster." The song was first released on Kanye's website before the album came out. "Monster" features Rick Ross, Jay-Z, and Nicki Minaj. The song also features Justin Vernon from the indie rock band Bon Iver. The song made it to number 18 on the singles chart.

My Beautiful Dark Twisted Fantasy was a big success. In the week the album came out, it was the number-one album in the United States. That week, the album sold almost 500,000 copies. It was less than Kanye had sold in the past, but was one of the biggest albums of the year.

Kanye didn't slow down in 2011. In the summer, he and rapper Jay-Z released an album together. The two rappers called their album *Watch the Throne*. The album was a big hit. *Watch the Throne* was one of the most successful albums of 2011. Jay and Kanye toured the world together, calling themselves the Throne. Fans loved to see two of rap's biggest artists working together to make great music.

Looking to the Future

In just a few years, Kanye went from music fan to music maker. A few years later, he went from popular producer to hip-hop's next big thing. Kanye used that chance to become one of the biggest stars in hip-hop. Though he's done things that have made people mad, he's still on top of the music world. Today, Kanye West is one of music's most well known names.

After *My Beautiful Dark Twisted Fantasy* and *Watch the Throne*, the future was wide open for Kanye. Kanye had shown the world that he makes great music, even though he sometimes makes mistakes. And making music is all Kanye's ever wanted to do. He's been chasing his dreams in music for years. Now that he's reached his goals, what comes next is anyone's guess.

1977 Kanye West is born on June 8 in Atlanta, Georgia.

1997 Coproduces tracks for Harlem World and Mad Rapper.

2002 Tells Oprah Winfrey that he'll be on her show one day

    Involved in a near-fatal car accident.

2004 First CD, *The College Dropout*, is released.

2005 Appears on *Oprah* and Barbara Walters's *Most Fascinating People of the Year*

    Releases *Late Registration*

    Kanye West Foundation program Loop Dream is introduced into five schools

    Wins five Grammy Awards

    Chicago mayor declared February 27 Kanye West Day.

    Receives the Million Man March Image Award

    Performs at Live 8 concert in Philadelphia

    Appears on the cover of *Time* magazine

    Goes "off-script" to criticize President Bush during an NBC telethon for hurricane relief; he repeats his comments a few days later on Ellen DeGeneres's show.

2006 Appears as Jesus Christ on the cover of *Rolling Stone*

    Wins three Grammy Awards.

2007 Kanye releases *Graduation* on September 11, alongside 50 Cent's *Curtis*. The two have had a long-time rivalry; 50 Cent thought Kanye moved his release date to the same day as him to compete for sales, while Kanye claims it was to give the world twice the amount of great music.

2008 His Glow in the Dark Tour starts in April and continues into 2009.

2009 Kanye West infamously interrupts Taylor Swift's first VMA award speech. He takes the microphone from her hand and says Beyoncé should have won.

2010 Kanye's next album, *My Beautiful Dark Twisted Fantasy*, is released

Rapper Vincent Peters sues Kanye for stealing "Stronger" from him.

2011 Kanye West and Jay-Z release *Watch the Throne*.

In Books

Baker, Soren. *The History of Rap and Hip Hop*. San Diego, Calif.: Lucent, 2006.

Comissiong, Solomon W. F. *How Jamal Discovered Hip-Hop Culture*. New York: Xlibris, 2008.

Cornish, Melanie. *The History of Hip Hop*. New York: Crabtree, 2009.

Czekaj, Jef. *Hip and Hop, Don't Stop!* New York: Hyperion, 2010.

Haskins, Jim. *One Nation Under a Groove: Rap Music and Its Roots*. New York: Jump at the Sun, 2000.

Hatch, Thomas. *A History of Hip-Hop: The Roots of Rap*. Portsmouth, N.H.: Red Bricklearning, 2005.

Websites

Kanye Fast Site
www.kanyelive.com

Myspace: Kanye West
www.myspace.com/kanyewest

Official Kanye West
www. kanyewest.com

Discography
Albums

2004   The College Dropout

2005   Late Registration

2007   Graduation

2008   808s & Heartbreak

2010   My Beautiful Dark Twisted Fantasy

2011   Watch the Throne (with Jay-Z)

Index

About the Author

C.F. Earl is a writer living and working in Binghamton, New York. Earl writes mostly on social and historical topics, including health, the military, and finances. An avid student of the world around him, and particularly fascinated with almost any current issue, C.F. Earl hopes to continue to write for books, websites, and other publications for as long as he is able.

Picture Credits